Growing Unusual Vegetables

PENN

C000147639

Contents

Introduction

Most gardeners, even those who have no more space than a small window box or a few flower pots in a drab back yard, usually attempt to grow something to eat. There is a pride in home-grown food that brings out the flavour better than any sauce.

It certainly pays to grow your own, but perhaps even more important is the quality factor. Nothing you will buy ever tastes as good as the food that comes straight from your own garden and is fresh, undamaged and, one hopes, unpolluted.

If you plan to grow your own vegetables and salads, why not grow those that are hard to get (except during a very short season) and, as a consequence, often very expensive? If you have a freezer you will be able to preserve many of these crops in bulk, and eat them in the depths of winter when your neighbours are boiling their third lot of frozen sprouts that week.

So often vegetables are regarded as something served up as a bit of padding around the meat, and are boiled and bashed to the point of disintegration. This is a great pity. The value of overcooked food is nil. Vitamins are often fugitive substances that vanish into thin air at the first touch of heat.

But you don't have to be a fervently committed vegetarian to savour the delights of fresh bean sprouts, or succulent blanched chicory wrapped in bacon with a velvety white sauce.

Certainly, the more unusual your vegetables the more you will be able to enlarge your range of recipes, bringing to the table novelty and interest instead of the 'usual' dishes.

One of the great values of these unusual vegetables must be their appearance. Often they look striking in the garden, worthy of a position where they can be seen from the house. Globe artichokes and cardoons are particularly spectacular and look splendid at the back of a border.

The Jerusalem artichoke makes a good screen during the summer months, growing into a dense hedge or thicket from 2 to 3m (6 to 10ft) high. In the autumn the leaves fall, but the tubers are available for hot soups.

Fennel is another decorative plant; there is a purple or bronze form which is usually used as a border plant though it is perfectly suitable for the table as well.

It is a mistake to assume that the rarer vegetables are harder to grow or need more special treatment than the usual ones. With the exception of asparagus, which takes a lot of time to get ready and monopolizes a large part of the garden for years, most of the plants described are easy and resilient.

Dandelions, for example, are so easy and so resilient that they are harder to get rid of than to grow, but provided they are carefully kept from seeding they will not take over the rest of the garden. It is well worth the effort, since few plants are as versatile as this one.

One or two of these plants need more warmth than is found in Britain in an average summer, but these can normally be grown in a greenhouse or indoors on a warm, south-facing windowsill.

I have assumed only a slight knowledge of gardening on the part of the reader. Where a special fertilizer or drainage is required I have said so. But by and large any ordinary gardener should be able to grow these 'unusual vegetables'.

Jerusalem artichoke

Fennel

Dandelion

Globe Artichoke

The globe artichoke probably originated in the Mediterranean region where it was known to the Greeks and Romans.

Someone must have had a particularly enquiring mind, since at first sight there is little in a 1.5m (5ft) high thistle to suggest that any of it can be eaten.

The edible part is the fleshy area at the base of the scales or bracts as shown in the drawing.

Globe artichokes need an open and sunny site where the soil is rich and well drained, otherwise small tough flower heads will form.

Buy young plants or suckers in April and plant out 1m (3ft) apart in each direction. The new plants may need some shading until they are well established. In May put a mulch of compost or manure around the plants.

Remove all flower buds as soon as they appear in the first year, in order to encourage stronger growth in the second and subsequent years.

In their second and third years allow each plant to develop only four to six stems. Mature plants should have ripe flower heads on

Globe artichoke

4

them ready to pick by July. Pick them when they are green and tightly bunched up, starting with the largest.

Normally, plants are replaced after four years either with new plants or with shoots cut from the old plant. These shoots must retain a portion of root. If this is done in April the shoots can be planted out in their final positions. The old plant must be discarded.

Although normally grown as an edible plant the globe artichoke is handsome in its own right and worthy of a place in the ornamental garden, but remember, it needs a lot of room.

Immature flower head

Pests and Diseases
Few problems beset the globe artichoke. In wet years slugs may be a nuisance and slug pellets are the best deterrent.

The major ailment is petal blight, the symptom of which is dark spots on the petals. The flowers ultimately rot. Spray with Zineb and destroy affected flowers.

Uses
To prepare for cooking, trim the stalk level with the base of the flower head, and slice off the top and any damaged outer scales. Trim the remaining scales with scissors and remove the choke (the hairy purple bit inside).

Cooked flower head

Boil the heads for 40 minutes in a pan of water to which salt and two tablespoons of lemon juice have been added. They are tender when the scales can be easily pulled away.

Turn them upside-down to drain and serve hot with melted butter or cold with a French dressing.

Jerusalem Artichoke

This is in no way related to the globe artichoke, nor is it from Jerusalem. It is related to the sunflower, and 'Jerusalem' is probably a corruption of *girasole*, the Italian name for the sunflower.

It was brought back from America in the seventeenth century but never caught on—unlike its fellow tuber (completely unrelated), the potato.

Almost any kind of soil can support a row of Jerusalem artichokes and I have seen them grow up to 2.5m (8ft) in a three-month drought. The tubers, however, were puny and riddled with holes. It pays, therefore, to prepare the ground for them.

In February or March make a furrow about 150mm (6in) deep and plant the tubers 455mm (18in) apart. If preferred they can be planted this deep in holes made with a trowel.

Each part of the knobbly tubers will sprout from its 'eyes', so you can plant a longish row from a few tubers by simply breaking them up; though small ones, about the size of a small hen's egg, are better planted whole.

In an exposed site you may need to stake the plants otherwise the wind will blow them over. Little else is required since they grow very tall and quickly smother weeds. (Few plants hide dustbins as well as artichokes in the summer!)

Harvest from October onwards all through the winter. Leave the stems in the ground after the tops have died off, to mark the tuber's position. Unless you want another crop to spring up make sure that you harvest every bit from each plant.

Pests and Diseases

Cutworms or wireworms may eat into the tubers. Apply Diazinon in the soil. Slugs sometimes eat into the tubers and the cure for this is a scattering of slug pellets around the base of the plants.

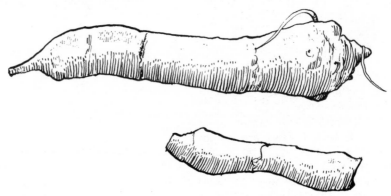

Artichoke tubers

Uses

The flavour of Jerusalem artichokes has an earthy quality not to everyone's taste. It is important to use the tubers as soon as they are taken from the ground since the delicate, truffle-like perfume vanishes after about an hour leaving merely a sweetish potato flavour.

They should be cleaned, peeled, par-boiled and then sliced and fried in hot olive oil or roasted around a joint. Creamed, they make a pleasant soup.

Here is a recipe that I think is the best I have tried. There could be many variants on it.

Jerusalem Artichokes with Tomatoes

Artichokes
Salt
Olive oil
Tomatoes
Dried marjoram
Garlic
Black pepper

Peel and clean the artichokes, and simmer in salted water until they are almost cooked. Remove from the pan and halve each tuber. Heat a little olive oil in a frying pan and add the tubers. For each $\frac{1}{2}$kg (1lb) of tubers add two skinned and chopped tomatoes and dried marjoram chopped with garlic. Add salt and freshly ground black pepper. When the tomatoes have been reduced to a pulp the dish is ready to eat, either by itself or with meat.

Jerusalem artichoke

Asparagus

This plant is a native of Europe and grows wild on sea shores. There are no great problems involved in its cultivation but the main drawback for the average gardener is the time which its cultivation takes.

It has a cropping season of only about six weeks but monopolizes its bed all the year round.

Despite all this many people resent the high prices that they have to pay for these succulent shoots and prefer to play the waiting game.

When you have decided where the bed is to be, bearing in mind that it may be there for fifteen or more years, dig in manure or compost in the autumn at a bucketful to the square metre. At the same time remove every trace of weeds. It helps to raise the bed by about 600mm (2ft) if the soil is sticky or badly drained.

Leave the bed until spring, letting the frost break it down, and then rake the soil, working in a general fertilizer. If it is acid, add lime.

You can grow asparagus from seed but this will add an extra year on to your waiting time. For quicker results buy two-year-old roots or crowns and plant from early to mid-April. Take out a trench 300mm (12in) deep, and wide enough to allow the roots to spread. The rows should be 1m (3ft) apart. Make the bottom of the trench raised in the centre (see drawing). Place the plants 450mm (18in) apart and cover the roots with about 75mm (3in) of soil. The trenches should gradually fill up as the summer's cultivations are carried out, hoeing and drawing the soil up from the sides.

Keep the bed well weeded and watered for two years and in autumn cut down the yellowing leaves or ferns and mulch well

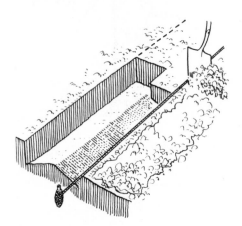

Asparagus bed

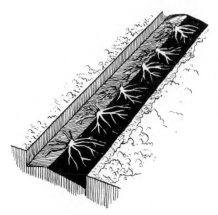

Asparagus planted on ridge

with well-rotted manure or compost. Do not harvest until the plants are three years old and then only three sticks (the young shoots) per plant.

In subsequent years harvest alternate sticks allowing the previous year's crop to grow on into ferns. A bed cropped like this might remain very productive for up to twenty years.

Harvest the shoots when their tips are about 100mm (4in) above the soil, using a special asparagus cutter or a serrated knife and cutting the base of the shoot, which will be about 100mm (4in) *below* the soil.

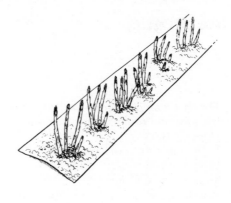

Asparagus

Uses

Having waited all this time for the shoots, what do you do with them? The important thing is, they must be fresh. They do freeze, but frozen asparagus is second best.

They are best cooked simply. Wash them, taking care not to damage them. Trim off any woody parts at the bases. White stems must be peeled off from the tip downwards. Trim the ends so the spears are all the same length and tie them into bundles with thin string. Stand the bundles upright in a pan of salted boiling water for about 10 minutes; the time depends on their thickness. The tender tips will cook in the steam.

They can then be served hot or cold.

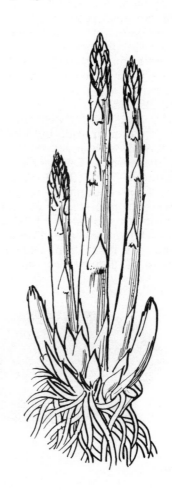

Aubergine

This is a native of tropical Asia and therefore a greenhouse or indoor plant in Britain.

In the south of England, however, I have grown quite sizeable fruits outside against a south-facing wall, in a very sheltered spot. Try them outside if you like but be prepared for failure.

There are two types that look rather different. The one most often seen in greengrocers is the deep purple, marrow-shaped one. The other, from which I suspect it gets its name 'egg-plant' is white and egg-shaped.

Indoors you should get about 10 fruit on a plant but outdoors the number will be far smaller.

Sow the seed in February at a temperature of 18°C (64°F). When they are large enough to handle prick them out into small pots and grow on in a temperature of 16°C (61°F). When they are 150mm (6in) tall put them into 180mm (7in) pots of John Innes No 2.

Pinch out the growing tip of each plant when it is about 230mm (9in) tall in order to encourage bushy growth and allow three fruits to form (if they will) on each lateral branch. Feed once a week when the fruit are developing and spray the leaves frequently to discourage red spider.

Pests and Diseases

Aphids may be a problem but they should be easy to deal with in a greenhouse. Red spider mites will multiply if you do not keep the atmosphere humid. Spray also with derris or malathion.

Uses

Aubergines are ripe when they are either all-over blackish purple or creamy white depending on the variety. They should be very glossy and a prod with the finger should leave a permanent mark.

To take away the slight bitterness, slice and sprinkle with salt. This is left on them for 30 minutes in order to absorb the bitter juice. After this they can be rinsed and dried. If you are stuffing the aubergines, just cut them into halves before salting.

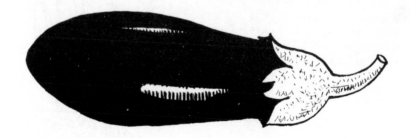

Aubergine

Here is a recipe for moussaka; there are many variations.

Moussaka

3 or 4 aubergines
1 large onion
Olive oil
450g (1lb) minced beef or lamb
1 tablespoonful chopped parsley
Medium tin of tomatoes
$\frac{1}{2}$ pint bechamel sauce
1 egg
Salt and pepper

Fry the sliced aubergines in olive oil until tender, adding more oil if they dry up. Remove them from the pan. Fry the sliced onions in the oil and add the meat. Continue cooking until brown. Add the tin of tomatoes, season with parsley, salt and pepper, and simmer for 30 minutes until most of the liquid is absorbed.

Make the bechamel sauce in the usual way and remove from the heat. Beat in the egg and pour this sauce over the aubergine layers.

Place a layer of cooked aubergine slices in an oven-proof dish and cover with a layer of mince. Continue making alternate layers, finishing with aubergines. If you wish, sprinkle with Parmesan cheese. Then bake in a warm oven (18°C, 350°F, gas mark 4) for 45 minutes or until the top is nicely browned.

Aubergine plant

Beans

Unusual vegetables? Certainly not the runner beans that grow in every other back garden in Britain. Nor the broad bean, well known to gardeners since the Iron Age. But have you ever tried to grow haricot beans, soya beans or sprouting bean shoots?

Haricot beans are eaten by the ton every day, heavily disguised as 'baked beans', normally in tomato sauce. They can, however, be picked when the pods are green and juicy, and eaten whole, or they can be dried in the pod and then reconstituted with water to make soups and stews.

Haricot beans are varieties of French or kidney beans. They are normally grown in warmer countries, where they are ripened in the pod and often form a staple food.

French Beans need a light, well-drained soil and sunny position out of rough wind. During the autumn before sowing, the soil should be thoroughly dug and enriched with well-rotted manure or compost.

Sow in succession after the last frost has gone—usually about mid-May. Sowings can be made from then until early July. Each 'station' should be 200mm (8in) apart, and two seeds should be sown 50mm (2in) deep at each station. If they both germinate, you will need to remove the weaker one, so do not plant them too close together. They may need some support later.

Soya beans are sown in the

Soya bean plant and pods

same way, though closer together as they do not branch out like French beans. The crop depends very much on the weather, more so than in the case of French beans. In a cool, dull summer you may get nothing at all.

On the credit side, however, soya beans are probably the most nutritious food available, rich in protein and vitamins.

If you are lucky enough to get a good crop, they can be eaten in the pod, or shelled, or dried and stored.

Beans in jam jar

Bean Sprouts

Sprouting beans and other seeds have been an important item of diet for over 4,000 years. Even if you have no garden, not even a window box, you can still eat green shoots full of health-giving vitamins and trace elements.

For bean sprouts one normally uses mung beans or adzuki beans which can be bought from a local health store or often at the local supermarket.

Fenugreek is suitable for curries and has a musky curry-like taste and smell.

Wash the seeds, beans, fenugreek, or cereal in several changes of water, and soak them for some hours. Then place them in a large jar.

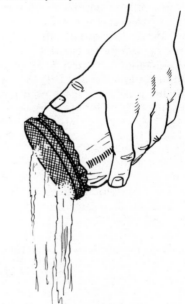

Emptying water from jar

Cut a piece of muslin that will fit over the top of the jar and secure it with an elastic band. Fill the jar with cold water every day, and then empty it, leaving the seeds wet and clean. Keep it in a dark, warm place. The seeds will soon burst and the tiny white shoots will appear.

Cook bean sprouts the Chinese way by frying in very hot oil, stirring all the time. Serve them hot, crisp and crunchy.

Shoots

Capsicum

This plant came originally from tropical America and is normally grown indoors in Britain. In a good year they will fruit well in the south and west of England.

The capsicum or sweet pepper is also called paprika. Another plant of the same group is the chilli, used to impart its often violent pungency to curries.

Sow seeds in March at a temperature not lower than 16°C (61°F), either in a pan of seed compost or (better) in individual pots or blocks. The final potting out (after all danger of frost is over) should be into 230mm (9in) pots of John Innes No 3 compost and canes should be inserted to support the plants.

When flowers appear, spray them with water every day to assist in setting the fruit, and feed regularly with a liquid feed such as Phostrogen. Each plant ought to support about six fruits, which you can pick green or red.

Pests and diseases
If white fly is a problem, treat with Malathion.

Uses
Sweet peppers, washed and cut into strips, add colour to a salad and have a crisp sweetness all

their own. They are very rich in vitamin C when eaten raw.

They are particularly good stuffed with rice, as in the following recipe.

Stuffed Peppers
2 large peppers (any colour)
57g (2oz) long-grain Patna rice
Small onion
Clove of garlic
A few coriander seeds
Pinch of dried basil
Tablespoon parsley
Tablespoon currants
Tablespoon pine nuts (if available)
Olive oil
Salt and pepper

Boil the rice for about 10 minutes and drain it when it is almost, but not quite, soft.

At the same time, fry the sliced onion in the oil, adding the crushed garlic, coriander seeds, basil and salt and pepper to taste. Simmer gently for about 15 minutes, then mix with the drained rice. Add the currants, parsley and pine nuts.

Cut the peppers in half lengthways and remove the projections and seeds. Then fill the halves with the mixture, making it raised towards the centre. Place the peppers in an ovenproof dish and add one tablespoon of olive oil to each half. Cover the dish and cook in a slow oven (135°C, 275°F, gas mark 1) for 1½ hours.

They are delicious either hot or cold.

The same mixture can be used for stuffing tomatoes, though in this case the juice and seeds of the tomato are added to the mixture.

Sweet pepper

Cardoons

The cardoon is a close relative of the globe artichoke. It is grown not for its globes but for the tender midribs and stalks of the young leaves.

They are hardly ever grown in this country, and for the gardener who wants to try out unusual vegetables a couple of these very handsome and decorative plants would be enough.

Their culture is similar to that of globe artichokes, except that they are always raised from seed. They are sown in April where the plants are to grow, or in March under glass.

As the plants grow they must be well supplied with water and they benefit from a weekly feed with a liquid fertilizer throughout the summer.

By the end of September the plants are ready for blanching. This should be done on a dry and sunny day when both the soil and the plant are dry. Tidy up the plant, removing any dead or dying leaves, and then gather up the foliage into a bunch, tying it as in the drawing.

Cardoon

Next wrap brown paper or black polythene sheeting around each plant (see drawing), and tie this with string or raffia. Earth up the plants. After about a month the blanching should be complete and you can harvest the plants as they are needed. In frosty weather they should be covered with straw or bracken, though you may prefer to lift all the plants by November and store them, still wrapped up, in a cool dry place.

Uses

The stems have an artichoke flavour and can be used in much the same way as celery, though they are not suitable for eating raw. They should be cleaned, removing any stringy parts, and can be left in a bowl of water to which lemon juice has been added in order to prevent discoloration before cooking. Cook the stems in boiling salted water until tender, about 20 minutes.

They may then be drained and served with butter, or they can be coated with a bechamel or cheese sauce.

The flavour of cardoon is delicate, and it should be cooked carefully to preserve its flavour, as can be seen from the advice contained in Vilmorin-Andrieux's book *The Vegetable Garden*, published in 1885:

'Cooked in a delicate way, it is excellent, but with the ordinary cook this, like many another good vegetable, is often spoiled. The degree of tenderness to which it is boiled should be studied, and the sauce should not be rank with salt and spice after the vulgar fashion.'

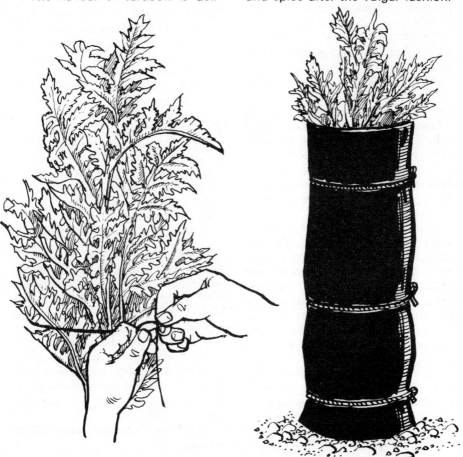

Tie up plants and wrap in paper

Celeriac

This is sometimes known as turnip-rooted celery, which describes the plant exactly. The flavour is that of celery and the roots make an excellent substitute for it. Celeriac is, however, a great deal easier to grow than trenched celery. Few ordinary gardeners have the time to fuss with blanched celery, and self-blanching celery is often a poor substitute with a watery flavour.

Prepare the plot by digging in plenty of well-rotted manure or compost in the autumn at a rate of a bucket per square metre. Next spring, work the soil to a fine tilth. In mid-March sow seeds either in the greenhouse or on a sunny window sill, and when the seedlings are big enough to handle prick out to 40mm (1½in) apart.

Plant out in May 350mm (12in) apart in rows the same distance apart. As the plants grow keep them well supplied with water, and mulch if necessary in a drought. Keep free of weeds and remove any side growths that may appear. Keep the bulbous root tops covered, otherwise they will turn green.

Lift the roots as required from the end of October. All of them should be lifted and stored in damp sand before the first frosts.

Pests and Diseases

These are the same as for celery—celery fly, carrot fly, slugs and snails. Leaf spot is the principal ailment, caused by bacteria and fungi which produce brownish spots on the affected leaves. Remove the diseased parts and spray plants with a fungicide such as Captan.

Uses

If the roots are small, about ½kg (1lb) in weight, they may be tender enough to eat raw. Cut them into thin slices and then into sticks like matchsticks. These can be incorporated into a salad with a French dressing.

Here is a good warming soup for a winter's day.

Celeriac Soup

450g (1lb) celeriac
2 leeks
1 large onion
57g (2oz) butter
1.2 litres (2pt) stock
Salt and pepper
Parsley and chives for garnishing

Scrub the celeriac and cut off all bits of root and leaf. Peel and cut into small pieces. Clean the leeks, then chop them finely. Peel and chop the onion.

Melt the butter and gently soften the chopped vegetables in it. Add the stock, season well and then simmer until the vegetables are tender. Put the soup through a sieve or liquidizer and then re-heat adding a little milk.

Serve with chopped chives and parsley.

Celeriac

Scrubbing celeriac

Grating celeriac

19

Celtuce and Lettuce Freaks

Celtuce

This is essentially a lettuce. The odd name reflects the hopes of seedsmen that this might become accepted as a dual-purpose plant, but this has not happened, since the similarity to celery seems a bit fanciful.

The leaves can be eaten like ordinary lettuce leaves and in this respect are neither better nor worse than more conventional plants. The fat, juicy stem is, however, a worthwhile addition to a salad.

Lettuce Freaks

One of the most useful lettuce freaks has been the non-hearting variety called 'Salad Bowl'. In a dry year a few plants of this will stand and give good leaves time and time again when all else has shot up and gone to seed. For a small family this plant has the advantage that you can take just as much as you need each time since the plant is left to grow more leaves after picking.

Lettuces are best grown on a well-drained site. Incorporate a general fertilizer before sowing, which should be done in succession from March to the end of July. Sow in shallow drills 305mm (12in) apart. Thin out as soon as

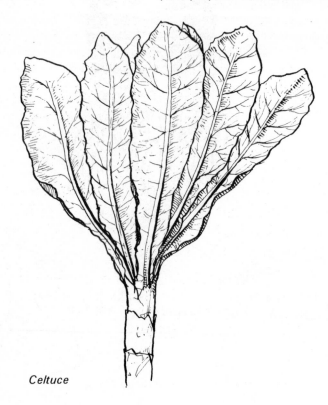

Celtuce

possible according to the size of the full-grown plant.

All lettuces prosper on a plentiful supply of water and many will bolt if they are dry for any length of time (except the non-hearting varieties).

Pests and Diseases

Aphids are one of the principal pests, more so in the case of hearting lettuce where, once they get into the plant, they are almost impossible to get out. You can avoid this by spraying your plants with one of the many aphid insecticides, or you can grow a non-hearting variety which seems to attract fewer aphids and is also easier to clean.

Useful as these non-hearting plants are, however, they do not have the flavour of some of the more conventional cos or cabbage types.

Uses

The heart of a good salad is usually a good lettuce. But have you ever tried lettuce soup? This utilizes lettuces that are starting to bolt.

Lettuce Soup

3 lettuces
0.57 litres (1 pt) chicken broth
0.57 litres (1 pt) milk
butter or cream
salt and pepper

Wash the lettuces and cut into thin strips. Put these ribbons in a saucepan with a little broth, and simmer gently, adding a little more broth, until they are soft. Sieve or blend the mixture. Return the resulting purée to the pan adding the rest of the broth and the milk. Season to taste. Before serving, add a knob or two of butter or a little cream.

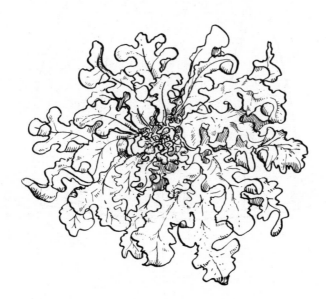

Salad Bowl

Chicory

A very useful hardy perennial plant all of which can be used, the roots as a coffee substitute or addition, the hearts (blanched) as a pleasant alternative to lettuce and the forced, blanched shoots in winter as a succulent cooked vegetable.

As a bonus, if it runs to seed the flowers are a very attractive blue, though it makes a very tall plant when fully grown. 'Witloof' is a variety cultivated for forcing in autumn, and the resulting blanched shoots are called 'chicons'.

'Sugarloaf' is a variety grown for its heart, which is eaten raw as a salad crop.

All varieties need the same initial preparation. In May, sow the seeds thinly in drills 5mm ($\frac{1}{4}$in) deep and 455mm (18in) apart. When the seedlings can be handled, thin them out to 250mm (10in) apart. Keep the weeds down by hoeing, and water well in dry weather.

When the leaves have died off in autumn, lift the roots carefully with a fork and cut off the remains of the leaves about 25mm (1in) above the root. Trim the roots to about 200mm (8in) and store them in a cool but frost-proof place until you need them for blanching.

Blanching is fairly simple. Put four of the roots in a pot that will

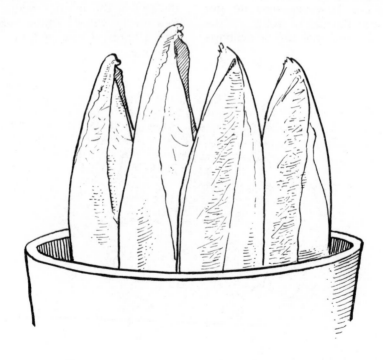

Chicory

easily hold them about 50mm (2in) apart when the pot is filled up with soil. Water the pot and then cover it with a fairly light tight cover. They should then be left in a dark warm place such as an airing cupboard.

In a few weeks the fat white shoots will begin to appear and should be harvested at about 150mm (6in) high. After this the roots should be thrown away, but you can try watering and covering them again. The second crop is generally poor, however.

Pests and Diseases

In the ground chicory may be attacked by slugs and snails or cutworms. When covered for forcing there is a danger of fungal growth which may spread and spoil the chicons.

Uses

The forced chicons can be eaten raw as part of a salad. Sometimes the centre is bitter and the larger older chicons are often too bitter to eat raw. This can be overcome to some extent by a short blanching; 2 minutes in boiling water is sufficient. Otherwise it can be cooked as in the following recipe.

Baked Chicory

4 chicons
4 rashers of smoked bacon
85g (3oz) grated cheese
Teaspoon of French mustard
Tablespoon butter
Tablespoon flour
0.28 litre ($\frac{1}{2}$pt) hot milk
Salt and pepper

Wrap the bacon around the chicons like a jacket. Place them side by side in a buttered ovenproof dish. Make the sauce by melting the butter, stirring in the flour and adding the milk slowly to avoid lumps.

Add most of the cheese and seasoning including the mustard. Cook in a medium oven (195°C, 375°F, gas mark 5) until the chicory is cooked. Then sprinkle the remaining cheese on top and brown under the grill.

This is a feast when served with fresh wholemeal bread.

If you want to try making coffee substitute or a powder that can be added to extend your real coffee, save the roots and dry them until brittle. Bake them in the oven until they will grind up in a coffee grinder. Dandelion roots can also be used for this purpose.

Chinese Cabbage and 'Chop Suey Greens'

Most seedsmen offer one or two varieties of Chinese cabbage often with exotic names. The plant called pak-choi or bok-choy is *Brassica chinensis* and is not closely related to the European cabbages. In Britain it runs to seed all too readily and should not be sown before July. It should be sown where it is to grow since it will not transplant.

Despite this, Chinese cabbage is well worth the effort since it has a delicate flavour and interesting texture if cooked the Chinese way.

Prepare the ground in late spring for a July sowing. Correct the soil's acidity if present with

Chinese cabbage

lime and spread compost or damp peat if the soil is dry.

Sow the seeds 12mm ($\frac{1}{2}$in) deep and thin out to 300mm (12in) apart as soon as the seedlings are large enough to handle. Make sure that they are well supplied with water at all times because once they start to bolt they are useless. In order to form a heart you may have to tie the outer leaves with raffia or twine.

Pe-tsai, wong bok and chihli are varieties of *Brassica pekinensis*.

Chop suey greens are chrysanthemum shoots, of which there are many varieties. The shoots have a powerful flavour and are to be used sparingly in combination with other food.

Pests and Diseases

The cabbages suffer from all the cabbage ailments and enemies; cabbage root-fly, for which bromorphos granules should be applied around the plants; and caterpillars or flea beetles, for which use derris.

Diseases include club root, which can only be avoided the next time round, since affected plants must be destroyed. To prevent it rotate crops, improve drainage if that is at fault, apply lime and put calomel dust in the planting holes.

Uses

Chinese cabbage is best cooked in the Chinese manner: that is, stir-fried in very hot vegetable oil with sliced beef and sliced mushrooms. The following is a good and simple recipe if you like sweet-and-sour mixtures.

Sweet and Sour Cabbage

1 Chinese cabbage chopped into thin ribbons
2 tablespoons oil
1 tablespoon salt
1$\frac{1}{2}$ cups of water
3 tablespoons sugar
3 tablespoons vinegar
1 tablespoon cornflour

Mix the sugar, vinegar and cornflour with one cup of water. Heat the oil and when it is very hot put in the chopped cabbage, stirring all the time for about a minute. Add the salt dissolved in the remaining $\frac{1}{2}$ cup of water, still stirring and after 2 minutes add the sweet-sour mixture. Keep stirring until the liquid becomes translucent. Serve at once.

Club root

Comfrey

A wild plant in this country, found in ditches and near rivers. It is hardly grown these days except by those who use it as 'green manure'. It can be composted or dug straight back into the soil. The value of comfrey in all this lies in the vast size of its leaves producing high amounts of nitrogeneous material. As much as 40 tons per acre has been reported.

Comfrey is easy to grow and difficult to get rid of, since any piece of the root, however small, will begin to grow. The roots will penetrate to a great depth, which

Comfrey

explains why it is so good as a green manure plant.

Ideally, establish comfrey in a shady and fairly damp site, giving the plants plenty of room to spread outwards and upwards. Once established they may be 1.2m (4ft) high, and correspondingly broad based.

When the plants are this large you may cut them down for green leaves. These can be used for composting and mulch in dry summer weather, and the small, tender ones can be eaten.

Uses

Comfrey can be used like spinach or any of the spinach substitutes such as spinach beet. Comfrey tea is a well-known herbal standby, and a poultice made from the pounded root was formerly used to hold together broken bones —hence one of its many common names, knitbone.

To make comfrey fritters, wash comfrey leaves with the stalks attached and then dip them into a thin batter made with egg, flour and water. Fry in deep fat for about two minutes.

Comfrey is a splendid potato fertilizer. Put a layer of cut comfrey into the trenches in spring before planting the seed potatoes. The resultant fertilizer is balanced and, best of all, very cheap.

Green manuring

Ideal plants for this purpose, such as comfrey, are deep-rooted and draw up minerals to the surface. Legumes such as tares are valuable because they 'fix' nitrogen in the soil where it can be taken up by the plants during the spring and summer. Tares can be sown from August to October and then dug in the following spring. Mustard is also used as a green-manure crop. It should be dug in when the first flowers are out.

If you want to try something different plant *Tagetes minuta,* a giant marigold. It grows to about 1.5m (5ft) high, kills eel-worm and smothers ground elder. However, it should be composted and not dug in as green manure since it is too tough.

Finally, weeds can be used as a source of green manure, before they are in flower. To do this hoe them down and leave them to rot in the soil.

The use of weeds in this way may be a new idea to some people. After all most sensible gardeners go out of their way to suppress any plant other than the one they are growing on the vegetable plot. Weeds compete for water, soil nutrients and light. Left alone the average vegetable garden would soon revert back to rough meadow land and the inbred cultivated plants would either revert to a more primitive form in order to survive or, much more likely, vanish.

Yet weeds are not different from 'respectable' plants. They often contain valuable elements that the soil in your garden lacks.

Taking nutrients from the soil in the form of huge cabbages and root crops and returning nothing is the quickest way to produce your own mini-desert. If weeds are allowed to grow, and then cropped, either for compost or hoed back into the soil, they can become an aid to better growing.

Courgette

I sometimes wonder, when I see a proud prizewinner holding a vast prize marrow, if these people ever eat the things. How much better those watery giants would have been if they had been nipped in the bud and picked when no longer than 100mm (4in) long. Then they are called courgettes, not marrows. Special varieties, such as 'zucchini', have been developed for cutting when immature.

Marrows are rich feeders, and grow extremely well on a compost heap. Failing this, dig out a sizeable hole where they are to be planted, and put in a bucketful of manure or compost. This should be done in May and the seed sown indoors at the same time. Sow two seeds in each pot or at each station in a tray 25mm (1in) deep. Remove the weaker of the two, if both germinate.

At the end of the month they should be ready to plant out in the prepared planting sites.

In a dull season, when few pollinating insects are about, you can increase the crop by transferring the pollen from male to female flowers with a soft brush, or by rubbing the male flower on to the female. The female flower is the one with the swelling behind it; this becomes the fruit when pollinated.

Courgettes

 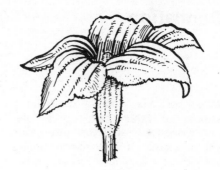

Courgette flowers (left) male (right) female

Pests and Diseases

Aphids can be a nuisance, so spray with malathion. Cucumber mosaic virus is usually transmitted by aphids so it pays to keep them down. In this disease the leaves and fruit become mottled and stunted. Plants must be destroyed as soon as you see this disease on them.

Uses

Courgettes should be cut and eaten when about 100mm (4in) long. At this size the seeds are immature and can be eaten, and the skin is soft. They may be cooked whole or sliced. In Southern France and Italy the flowers of the marrow are served stuffed, while in Mexico the yellow flowers are made into a soup. Here is a recipe for courgette soufflé.

Courgette soufflé

450g (1lb) courgettes
2 whole eggs
2 egg whites, beaten stiffly
5 tablespoons grated Gruyere cheese

Bechamel sauce made with $\frac{1}{8}$ litre ($\frac{1}{4}$pt) milk, 28g (1oz) butter, 2 tablespoons flour, pepper and salt.

Slice the courgettes into rings and then sprinkle them with salt. Leave them in a colander for an hour to remove all excess moisture.

Cook in a little water for about 10 minutes or until soft. Sieve them and stir the resulting purée into the bechamel sauce with most of the cheese. Remove from the heat and add the beaten eggs. Cool a little, then add the beaten egg whites.

Put into a buttered soufflé dish, sprinkle with grated cheese and then stand the dish on a baking tin containing water and bake at 180°C, 350°F, gas mark 4, for about 40–45 minutes.

Dandelion

Most of us grow dandelions sooner or later—not, as a rule, intentionally. In fact the new cultivated strains of this exceptionally useful and beautiful plant ought to be far more widely grown. They supply a constant harvest of leaves which when blanched make most lettuces taste weak. The roots can be dried, roasted and ground to make one of the few really good coffee substitutes there are, lacking caffeine which may be harmful and which certainly keeps a lot of

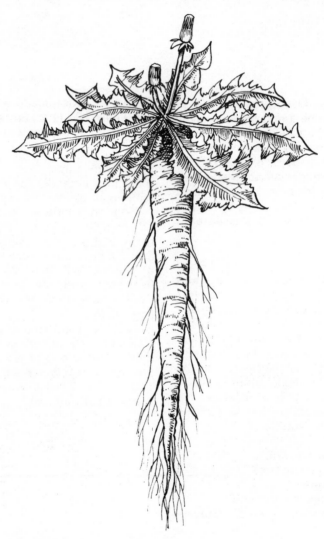

people awake at night. The flowers make one of the best country wines.

If you are brave enough actually to plant something which you may well have been trying to discourage for years, bear in mind that so long as you do not allow the seed heads to form, you need not fear an invasion.

Any garden soil will suffice though a little help with fertilizer will always produce bigger plants and better leaves.

Uses

To make a coffee substitute, scrub the roots and cut away any thin or rotten bits. Roast them in a fairly hot oven until they are brittle through and through but not carbonized. Then grind and use as coffee. The result is as good as average instant coffee, although neither resembles the real thing.

The leaves, which can be used in salads, must be well blanched with a large upturned flower pot otherwise they will be bitter. Don't forget to cover the hole.

Dandelion wine is a favourite of mine and a perfect way to stop the plants from seeding all over your garden.

This is a simple version.

Dandelion Wine

4.5 litres (1 gal) (volume) dandelion heads without stalks
1 orange
1 lemon
1.6kg (3½lb) sugar
4.5 litres (1 gal) water
7g (¾oz) bakers' yeast or a wine yeast

Put the flowers into the cold water and bring to the boil. Simmer for 10 minutes. Strain on to the sugar and the peel of the orange and lemon. Stir well, and when it has cooled slightly, add the juice of the orange and lemon. When it is lukewarm add the yeast mixed with some of the liquid. Cover with a cloth to begin fermentation. After 2 days put into a fermenting jar, insert an airlock and leave it to ferment to a finish. Let it age if you can.

Fennel

There are two sorts of Fennel in general use: common fennel, which is also a wild native plant in this country, and Florence fennel which is grown for its swollen leaf base, eaten as a raw salad vegetable.

The former is a perennial herb and is often grown as a decorative plant. There is a purple variety which is very attractive in the flower garden. Both plants are strongly reminiscent of aniseed in flavour.

Sow the seeds in March and thin out the plants to 305mm (1ft) apart when they are large enough.

Florence fennel is a trickier plant to grow because if it gets dry it will rush into seed, thus elongating and opening up the fat, tightly compressed stem base which is the part you want to use.

If this does happen, all is not lost: you merely have ordinary fennel instead.

Fennel

Florence fennel benefits from a soil that has been enriched the previous winter with compost or well-rotted manure. When the stem bases begin to swell up, draw the soil around them. Above all, ensure that they get plenty of water.

Pests and Diseases

Practically none, but if you are going to harvest the seeds you may find that a high proportion have beetles in them.

Uses

The ferny leaves can be cut as needed and may be chopped into salads, soups and any dishes where the fine aniseed flavour and perfume seem to be called for. If you do not pinch out the growing tip as the plants become tall, they will flower, and you will be able to harvest the seeds. These have a use in herbal tea-making and also in cakes. Bear in mind that the flavour is stronger in the seeds.

The stalks will dry out at the end of the season and may then be harvested and stored in a dry place. They can be used in many grilled meat and fish dishes.

Florence fennel may be cooked as a vegetable. Clean it, cut in half and then boil for about 20 minutes. Put the halves into a buttered fireproof dish. Sprinkle grated Parmesan cheese and breadcrumbs on top and bake in the oven until the cheese has melted.

Florence fennel

Good King Henry

This has the rather daunting Latin name of *Chenopodium bonus-henricus*. Both it and its relation, fat hen *(Chenopodium album)*, used to be popular before spinach took their place. Most of us have in fact seen these plants and others of the same group where there is disturbed ground, on bomb sites and by the roadside.

Fat hen was one of the staple foods of our Neolithic ancestors. In Saxon times, when it was called *melde,* villages were named after it, Melbourn in Cambridgeshire being one.

Both plants grow very easily. Their main use is as an alternative to spinach. Both are valuable foods, probably more nutritious than either cabbage or spinach.

Good King Henry can be grown almost anywhere though rich soil means bigger leaves. The leaves are fairly bitter. The buds can be picked in spring and lightly boiled, rather like sprouting broccoli, and the whole plant may be earthed up to elongate the main stems which can then be treated as asparagus.

Seed may prove difficult to obtain. The plant can be propagated from cuttings, however. As the plants develop you should cut back the foliage to encourage more bushy growth. Feeding helps to speed up the leaf growth-rate.

Uses

If these plants are used as a spinach substitute it is usually

Good King Henry

necessary to cook them in two lots of water to remove the bitterness. There are a few spinach recipes which use this bitterness to some effect, like the following, where the tang of bitter green offsets the creamy softness of the rest.

Good King Henry 'Florentine'
1 egg, poached
2 tablespoons boiled and chopped leaves

34

3 tablespoons double cream
Parmesan cheese
Salt and pepper

The leaves should be boiled and reduced to a purée, seasoned and put in a small ovenproof dish, the sort called a *cocotte* in France. Put a lump of butter in the middle and place the lightly poached egg on top. Pour over the cream and sprinkle with the cheese.

Bake in the oven until the surface is brown and crusty.

Other Spinach Substitutes

The trouble with spinach is that it tends to bolt (run to seed) in dry conditions and almost any summer has at least one such period however wet the season is overall.

Added to this is the fact that many true spinach varieties are low-growing and because of this the leaves become very muddy.

It is not surprising, therefore, that many people grow Spinach Beet or other substitutes. Spinach Beet is not a Spinach at all but a Beetroot which grows luxuriant thick leaves and has no swollen red root beneath. This most useful plant can be relied upon to provide leaves all through the summer into the frosts and even all through a moderate winter. In spring the plant puts out masses of new leaves but later it goes to seed.

It should be sown in drills 25mm (1in) deep and 230mm (9in) apart in good, rich, well-drained soil and then thinned to about 200mm (8in) apart. The resulting plants will grow quickly at first from a spring sowing, slowing down in winter. Leaves may be picked all through the season and a few plants would suffice for a typical family.

The flavour of Spinach Beet is coarse compared to real Spinach.

Nettles are often used, especially in rural areas, as a spinach substitute (although nettles have been with us a great deal longer than cultivated spinach).

The nettle has a long history of usefulness to man going back at least as far as the Bronze Age in Europe. It was used to make a thread from which cloth was woven. Mary, Queen of Scots is recorded as saying that bed sheets made from nettle fibre were better than linen. Sir Walter Scott had nettles grown under glass as a spring green.

Of course one of the first things you learn about nettles is that they sting. Even this was used to advantage in the past: it is said that the Romans found Britain so cold in winter that they are supposed to have stung their feet to make them feel warm. (I suspect this is a Celtic joke.)

You hardly need to grow them, though they were once deliberately cultivated. In spring, with gloves on, gather the young tips and cook them just as you would spinach. The sting vanishes on cooking. They have an earthy taste which I like but you may not.

You can also make beer from nettles and a sort of tea.

Another plant that may be used as a spinach substitute is Ground Elder, hardly a plant to introduce if your plot isn't infested with it but if it is you might as well eat it.

Chickweed can be eaten like cress, freshly chopped in sandwiches.

Kale

This is one of the toughest members of the cabbage family; kale can stand up to the hardest winters, thriving even when Brussels sprouts fall by the wayside.

Kale provides greens and vitamins during the coldest months from December through to April.

You can grow either plain- or curly-leaved kale. There is little difference in flavour. All kales are rather coarse. Of the curled varieties 'Pentland brigg' is very hardy, and of the plain-leaved ones 'cottager's kale' has the added interest of purplish leaves. 'Thousand headed' crops well in late winter.

Kale does best in an alkaline soil, so lime the plot after digging, as for all brassicas. Sow seed in April in a 12mm ($\frac{1}{2}$in) drill and thin to about 50mm (2in) apart.

In July, transplant the young plants to their final site, 610mm (2ft) apart. Firm in and water well at first. Depending on the variety, shoots can be cut from about Christmas onwards.

Kale, like broccoli, is vulnerable to wind during the winter gales. If left unaided the plants may fall over and the roots be left high and

Curly kale

Kale

dry. It is advisable to stake large and top-heavy plants if they seem to be rocking excessively.

Pests and diseases
The maggots of the cabbage-root fly may attack the roots after transplanting. Protect them with bromorphos granules around each plant.

Cabbage whitefly may attack the plants in winter; spray with Malathion or Pyrethum. Caterpillars may eat the developing leaves so that the plants eventually die. Pick them off by hand if possible, or spray with derris.

Club root is the danger disease of the cabbage tribe and affected plants must be burnt. Prevention involves improving drainage, the application of lime, and putting 4 per cent calomel dust in the planting hole. Above all do not grow members of the cabbage family on land that is known to be infected.

Uses
Kale is crisp, richly green during the grey end of the year, and high in vitamin C. When not too coarse, kale can be shredded raw as a winter salad. Discard the main ribs. To cook, boil in a small amount of salted water for about ten minutes. Drain, and serve the chopped leaves with melted butter and seasoning.

Kohl Rabi

This plant, sometimes called 'turnip-rooted cabbage', is eaten far more often on the continent than here—a great pity, since it has a lot to offer.

The flavour is between that of cabbage and that of turnip, though

Kohl rabi

perhaps nearer to the former. The edible part is not the root but the stalk which swells up into a ball. This should be harvested before it grows too large and woody. When it is the size of a tennis ball it is about right.

Since the kohl rabi matures in about twelve weeks or less, it makes a useful catch crop. It also survives the first frosts of the year. There are two colours, green or purple, but the flesh is white in both, and the flavour identical.

It does best in a rich and well-drained soil, and needs plenty of water if a supply of round succulent vegetables is wanted quickly.

Sow the seed starting in May. Do not transplant but ruthlessly thin out the seedlings to about 200mm (8in) apart. The rows ought to be 380mm (15in) apart. Keep well watered and weed-free.

Sowings may be made throughout the season up to August for a succession into winter.

Pests and Diseases

Unfortunately any of the cabbage family's many ailments may affect this plant. To combat aphids apply malathion, and to protect against cabbage-root fly, mix bromorphos or diazinon granules in the soil around each plant. Caterpillars should ideally be picked off, or sprayed with derris or malathion.

The main disease is club root.

Infected plants must be destroyed. To guard against club root, a serious and destructive fungal infection, apply lime to the soil before planting, make sure that the drainage is adequate, and put calomel dust into the planting holes. If all this fails, avoid growing any type of cabbage on this soil for a while.

Uses

When small and succulent, kohl rabi may be sliced and served raw with a French dressing. It is an interesting addition to salads.

It may be cooked in a variety of ways.

Peel 0.5kg (1lb) kohl rabi and cut into strips like potato chips. Boil these for about ten minutes in lightly salted water until they are tender but still firm. Drain and allow to cool. Melt 28g (1oz) of sugar in a heavy frying pan on a low heat until it melts and turns pale brown. Stir in 28g (1oz) of butter and keep on stirring until it is mixed with the sugar. Then put in the kohl rabi 'chips', stirring them carefully until all are coated with the golden caramel. Serve with a roast; it is especially good with pork, but bad for teeth!

A variation on this is to slice the kohl rabi much more thinly and then to 'stir fry' in the Chinese manner, as described for Chinese cabbage on page 24.

Onion Oddities

Most gardeners grow onions at some time, and the ordinary onion has a history at least as old as the pyramids.

There are, however, several 'offbeat' members of this large family, some of which can be growing all the year round to fill the gap left when your ordinary onions have gone or are beginning to sprout.

Others are worth growing simply because they are so odd. The tree onion, for example, is a perennial producing its bulbs up in the air, on top of its stalks. Another crop of little onions is down below, as in ordinary onions. This plant is sometimes called the Egyptian onion though it has nothing to do with Egypt.

The Welsh onion is also a perennial and will supply onion shoots all through an average winter. It grows in a tightly packed clump which needs to be split up every two years or so. Despite its name, the Welsh onion has little to do with Wales, having originated in Siberia. The word may be a corruption of *Welsche* which is German for 'foreign'. Other names are 'ciboule' and 'Japanese bunching onion'. It has been used in China and Japan for thousands of years. It makes a good substitute for the usual spring onion.

Chives are probably not unusual to most people, but should be included because they are so useful, especially in winter and spring when other types of onion may be

Tree onions

in short supply. The thin grass-like shoots can be cut all year round if you grow them in a pot and bring it indoors in winter.

One thing that all onions need is a sunny place in which to grow. They do best in a deep loam and are greedy feeders. The ground should therefore be well manured, though this is perhaps not as important for the onions described here as it would be for ordinary ones.

They need plenty of water while growing, and in a dry season you will have to water them often. Chives sometimes die away for lack of water despite their reputation as an invasive and rampant grower.

Uses

Chives can be chopped into soups or over salads—especially good with home-grown tomatoes and wine vinegar. Chopped chives can be put into bread which is then heated quickly in the oven; this is a variation on garlic bread, but is less potent.

All of these unusual onions are suitable for pickling if you have the patience to peel them.

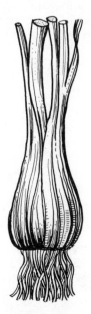

Welsh onions

Chives

Peas

There are several unusual varieties of peas, and at least one, the asparagus pea, is not really a pea at all. The French distinguish between peas for shelling and peas eaten in the pod. These last are called *sans parchemin*, that is, without the tough parchment-like layer in the pod.

The *sans parchemin* category includes the sugar pea and the mange-tout. These varieties are picked before the peas in the pods are fully developed and while the pod is soft and succulent. The entire pod is cooked.

Whatever the original differences between the sugar pea and the mange-tout, most seed merchants use the names interchangeably.

If you fancy a different colour you might consider growing purple-podded peas. They are a decorative sight in the vegetable garden since their height, about 1.5m (5ft), makes them particularly visible. Pods are long and the fairly small peas are not purple but green.

Petit pois, 'little peas', are miniatures although the plants are about 1m (3ft) tall. These must be shelled before eating.

Asparagus pea is sometimes called the winged pea because of the wing-like membrane that forms at the angles of the pods. The pods may be eaten when young and tender, or the seeds may be roasted and used as a coffee substitute.

The chick pea, like the asparagus pea, is not a true pea. It is grown for drying and is a valuable source of protein in winter. It is a Mediterranean plant and needs a bit of help in our colder climate.

Asparagus pea and pod

Start under glass and hope for a good summer otherwise the seeds will not ripen properly.

The pods should be left on the plants. A little before the first frosts, pull out the whole plant and hang it to finish drying in a shed. The dried peas need soaking overnight before use.

Uses

Dried chick peas and related legumes are used a great deal in Indian cooking as well as in Europe.

Here is a recipe from Persia.

Persian Meatballs
700kg (1½lb) minced beef or lamb
1 onion, finely chopped
Salt and black pepper
Oil
115g (¼lb) chick peas soaked overnight
450g (1lb) fresh spinach
1 tablespoon butter
2 cloves of garlic, crushed
1 teaspoon ground coriander

Make small meat balls with the meat, onion, salt and pepper. Fry in the oil until brown.

Boil the soaked and drained chick peas in water until soft. This may take from one to six hours according to age. Wash the spinach and remove thick mid-ribs. Drain well, chop the leaves finely, then stew them in their own juice with the butter until they are tender.

Add the drained and cooked chick peas and the meat balls and cover. Cook for about half an hour or until the meat balls are done. It may be necessary to add more water.

Crush two cloves of garlic with a little salt and then fry with the coriander for a couple of minutes. Add this to the meat balls and stir gently.

Serve with plain rice.

Chick pea and seeds

Salsify

This is one of those plants which might easily have become at least as well known and as commonly grown as the parsnip. It possesses a delicate flavour which has given it its other name of 'vegetable oyster'. Whatever the similarity may be, salsify is a lot cheaper than oysters!

The root is the edible part, and when digging them out you must be careful not to damage them, otherwise they will 'bleed'.

Salsify is a fairly easy plant to grow. It needs a deep soil that allows its long root to develop. Avoid growing it in ground that has just been manured, otherwise it will fork. Weeds are a problem since it is a slow grower and can easily be overtaken by other plants competing with it for light and moisture.

Sow in April, in drills about 375mm (15in) apart, and thin out to 250mm (10in) between plants. Don't let the plants go dry in hot weather.

The roots can be left in the ground until needed. They should be ready for use by October.

To prepare them for eating, scrub the roots, and wherever you cut them, rub the cut surfaces with lemon juice or put the cut pieces into a bowl of diluted lemon juice. This is to stop them going black. Any cooking method good for parsnips is right for salsify.

If you have a lot of plants, leave some to over-winter, and crop the

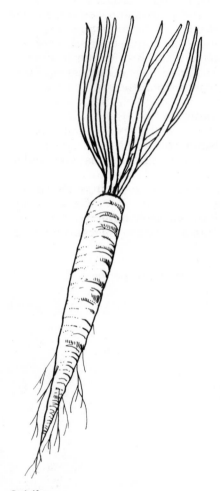

Salsify

tender new shoots in spring for early spring greens.

Scorzonera

This is sometimes called 'black' salsify, though it is not related. As with salsify, the long root is eaten. It should be treated like salsify, though in cooking it has one disadvantage: the skin has to be peeled off the parboiled root while it is still hot. This can be a finger-blistering operation and you may well wonder whether it is worth it.

An interesting point about scorzonera, however, is that the roots contain inulin which is a sugar allowed for diabetics. The root can also be used roasted as a coffee substitute.

Rampion

A similar vegetable that has all but fallen out of common cultivation, this is a native plant which grows well in Britain. The roots are white and crisp in texture and are eaten in salads, as are the leaves.

The seeds are very small indeed, in fact they are reputed to be the smallest of all vegetable seeds. A gramme contains more than 25,000 of them. It helps, when sowing, to mix the seed with saw-dust or sand. Sow in June to avoid the plant going straight to seed. It should be sown in drills about 300mm (12in) apart, the plants then being thinned to at least 100mm (4in) apart. Soil should be rich but light. Do not put the seed in too deep, and take great care, when watering, not to wash the lot away.

Lift the roots in autumn. They will keep in the ground until needed.

Rampion

Sweet Corn

Sweet corn ought to be grown far more widely. If you have once eaten it fresh you will not want to go back to shop-bought corn, and even less to the tinned variety.

Sweet corn originated in tropical America, and has had to be bred tougher in order to grow in Britain. But there are now many varieties that are fairly easy to grow here.

Prepare the ground during the previous autumn by digging in plenty of manure or compost. The site needs to be in full sun. When all likelihood of frost is past, sow the seed 12mm ($\frac{1}{2}$in) deep in rows

Sweet corn

500mm (20in) apart, leaving about 450mm (18in) between the plants.

As the plants develop, protect against birds, which sometimes pull out the young plants. The answer is to wind thin black cotton around sticks set amongst the stems. After tripping up a few times most birds lose interest. Do not use thick cotton or nylon since birds may get fatally tied up. The plants become tall and generally look after themselves. Do not hoe too close otherwise you may damage the surface-feeding roots. It is most important, especially in a drought, to keep sweet corn well watered, otherwise the cobs will not develop properly. The tall plants are easily blown over and if you have an exposed garden a little staking will help. It is important to harvest and use them at exactly the right time; this is when the tassel at the end turns brown.

Uses

Strip off the husk and boil the sweet corn until tender. Serve with butter. When you eat it fresh like this you will enjoy the sweetness that gives it its name, and which slowly vanishes as the cobs are kept.

There are a number of ornamental maize plants offered by seedsmen; these are not worth eating but are an attractive addition to the garden.

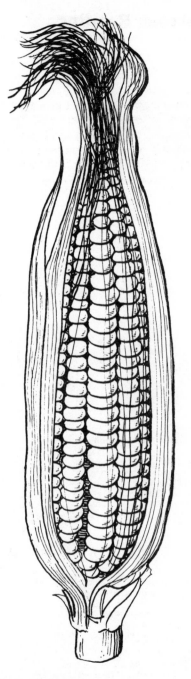

Corn on the cob

Further Reading

Food from your Garden (Reader's Digest, 1977)
Harrison, S. G. *et al. The Oxford Book of Food Plants* (Oxford University Press, 1969)
Mabey, Richard. *Food for Free* (Collins, 1972)
Sholto-Douglas, James. *Alternative Foods* (Pelham Books, 1978)
Vilmorin-Andrieux. *The Vegetable Garden* (John Murray, 1977) A facsimile of this classic which
  was first published in 1885, and a mine of information on plants which are now little-grown and
  little-known
Whitlock, Ralph. *Growing Unusual Vegetables* (EP, 1978)

Illustrated by Barry Gurbutt

Wilbur, Alan
Growing unusual vegetables.—(Penny pinchers).
1. Vegetable gardening.
I. Title II. Series
635   SB322

ISBN 0-7153-7904-6

Text and illustrations
© David & Charles Ltd. 1980

Printed in Great Britain
by A. Wheaton and Co. Ltd., Exeter
for David & Charles (Publishers) Limited
Brunel House Newton Abbot Devon